ALL MY FEELINGS

A Story for Children Who Have Felt The Impact of Crime or Trauma

Written by Debra Whiting Alexander, Ph.D.

Designed by Beth Weiner Lipson

ISBN 1-56688-055-6

PROMOTING GROWTH THROUGH KNOWLEDGE
135 Dupont Street, Plainview, N.Y. 11803-0760
1-800-99-YOUTH

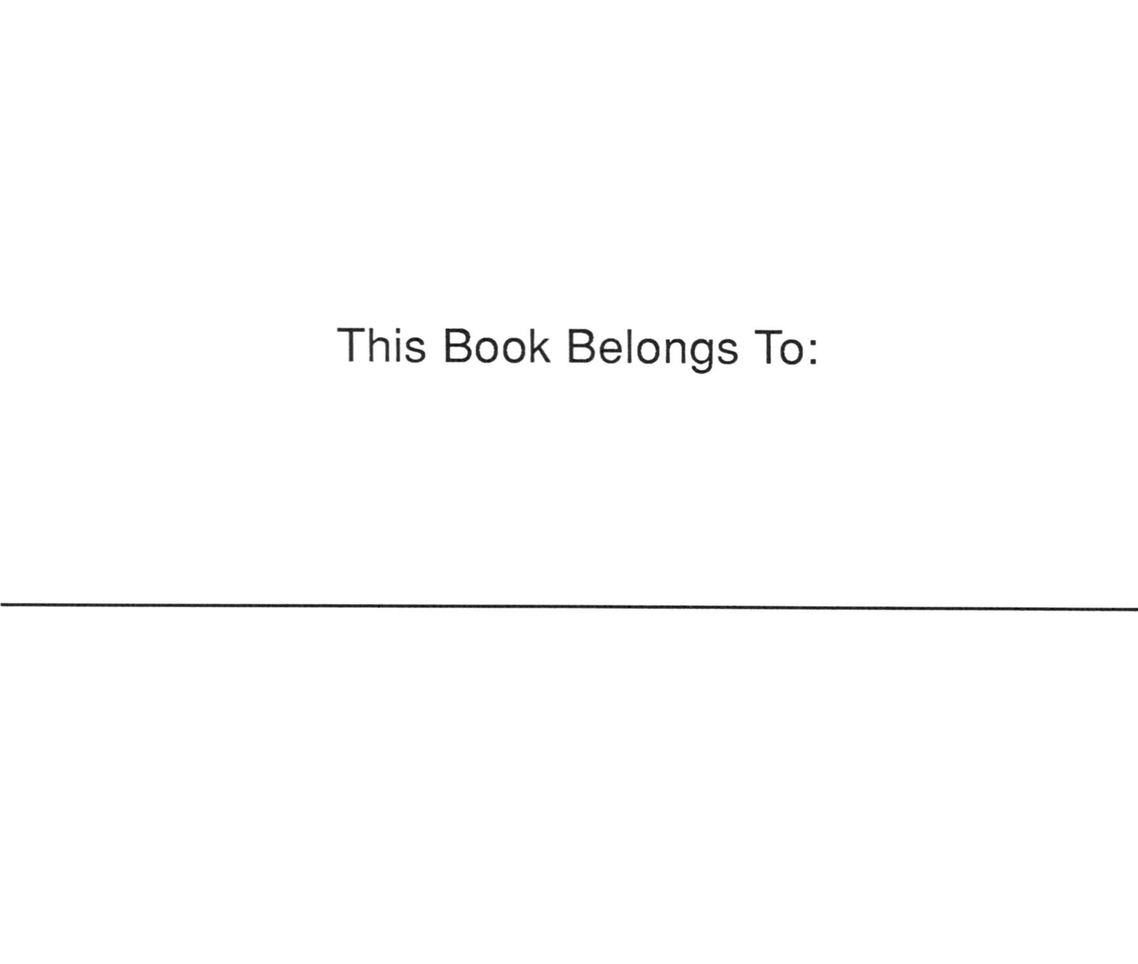
This Book Belongs To:

All my feelings have changed.

I learned that when bad things happen to people, the same kind of feelings happen to almost everyone. Some of those feelings are happening to me.

I feel all mixed up inside. My feelings come and go and sometimes they scare me. My feelings happen anywhere, at any time.

And, sometimes, I feel nothing at all.

I see a counselor. She said kids can have all kinds of feelings.

I found out feelings can't be right or wrong or good or bad. No matter what I think about, my thoughts and feelings can't hurt people or make bad things happen.

I am learning that I am the only one who can know all my feelings in the special way I do.

When I feel SHY, I don't want to talk. I stay quiet and listen. Feeling shy helps me know when I don't feel safe with someone or comfortable someplace. Feeling shy helps me know when I need more time.

When I Feel Shy

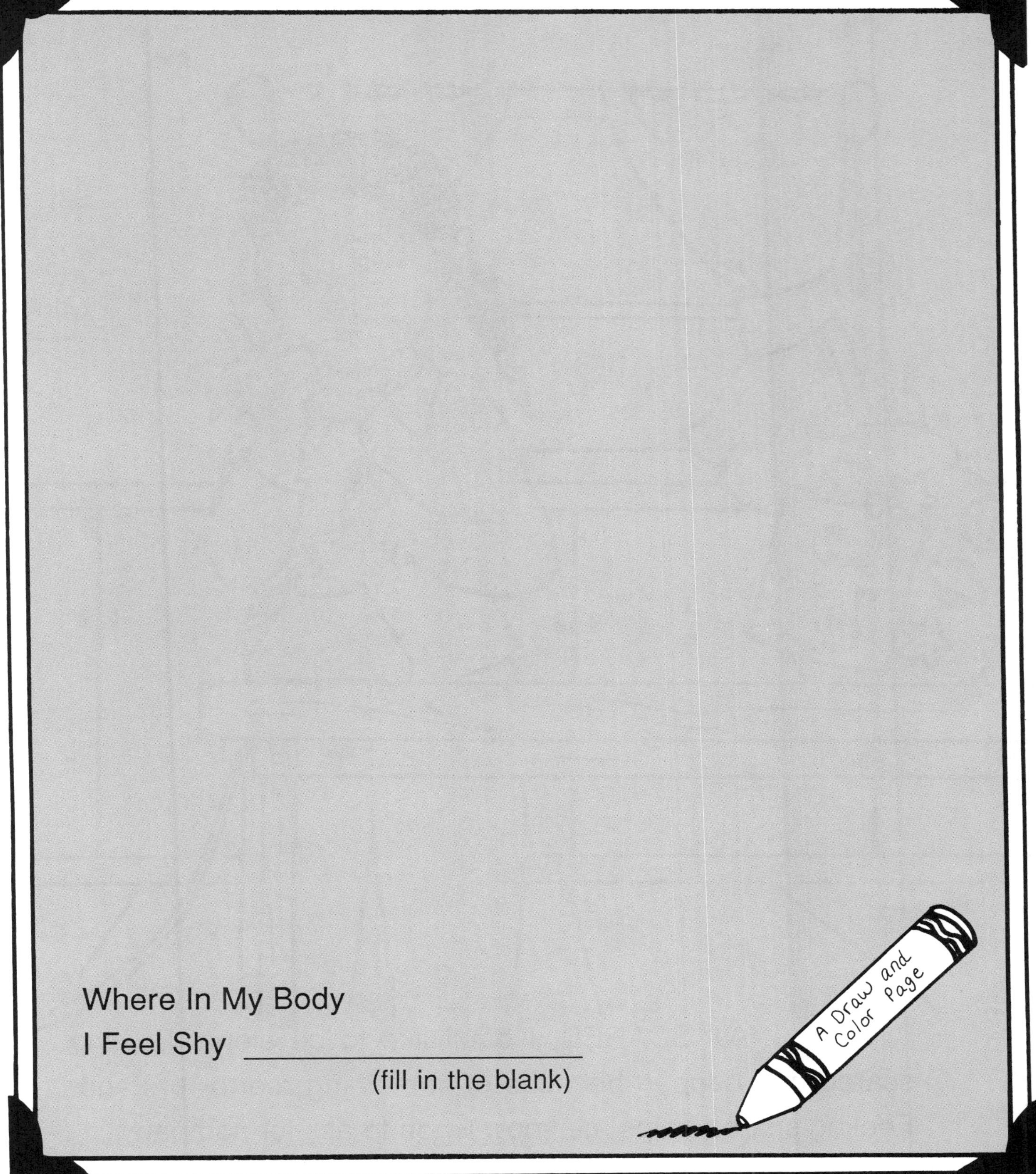

Where In My Body
I Feel Shy ____________________
(fill in the blank)

When I feel SCARED, I don't like to be alone. Feeling scared can happen because of something real or pretend. Feeling scared helps me know when to ask for company.

When I Feel Scared

Where In My Body
I Feel Scared ________________
(fill in the blank)

When I feel SILLY, I like to pretend. Sometimes I make up stories and songs with funny words. Feeling silly helps me to learn how to have fun with myself. It helps me to be new and different.

When I Feel Silly

Where In My Body

I Feel Silly ____________________

(fill in the blank)

When I feel ANGRY, I want people to know. Sometimes, I yell and want to hit. Sometimes, I just stop talking. When I need to, I can hit pillows because they have no feelings! Feeling angry helps me learn what I like and don't like. When I feel angry, I know somebody needs to listen to me.

When I Feel Angry

Where In My Body
I Feel Angry____________________
(fill in the blank)

When I feel SAD, I don't really want to smile. Sometimes, I feel sad when I miss someone I love, or when I feel lonely. Feeling sad helps me know when I need to talk, or cry, or be alone. Sadness helps me see what I'm needing.

When I Feel Sad

Where In My Body
I Feel Sad_______________________
(fill in the blank)

When I feel HAPPY, I like to smile and laugh. Sometimes, I jump and run. Feeling happy is fun! When I am happy, I learn what I enjoy about my life.

When I Feel Happy

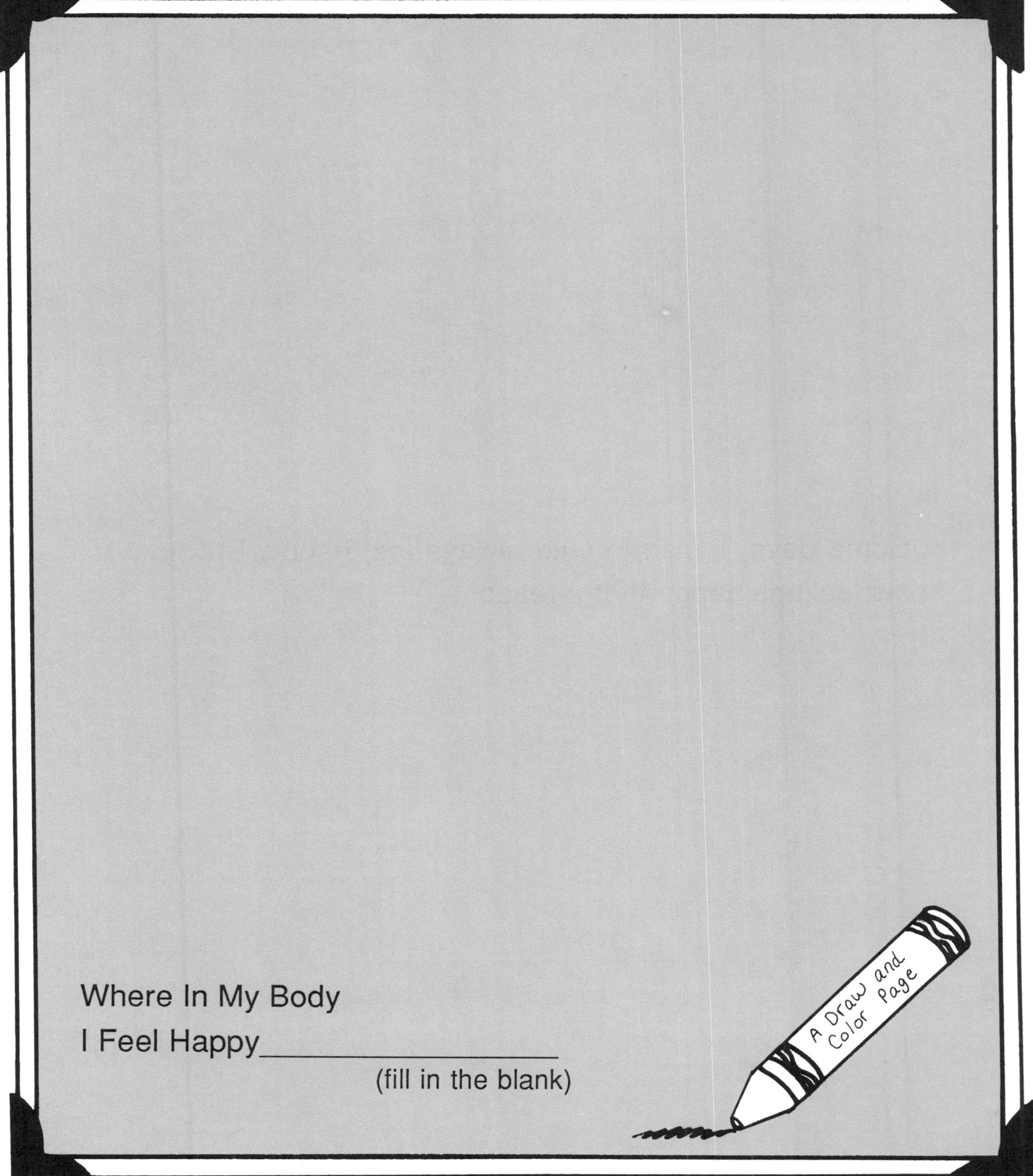

Where In My Body
I Feel Happy____________________
(fill in the blank)

Some days, I wish I could always feel happy. But now I know feelings happen for a reason.

Every feeling I ever have is a part of who I am. All my feelings are my friends.